T0104712

OBEDIENCE RATHER THAN SACRIFICE

OBEDIENCE RATHER THAN SACRIFICE

I Samuel 15:22 . . .
"Behold, to Obey
Is Better than Sacrifice"

Cinda M. Carter

authorHOUSE®

AuthorHouse™ LLC
1663 Liberty Drive
Bloomington, IN 47403
www.authorhouse.com
Phone: 1-800-839-8640

© 2014 Cinda M. Carter. All rights reserved.

No part of this book may be reproduced, stored in
a retrieval system, or transmitted by any means
without the written permission of the author.

Published by AuthorHouse 12/30/2013

ISBN: 978-1-4918-4394-9 (sc)
ISBN: 978-1-4918-4395-6 (e)

Library of Congress Control Number: 2013922937

Any people depicted in stock imagery provided by Thinkstock are
models, and such images are being used for illustrative purposes only.
Certain stock imagery © Thinkstock.

This book is printed on acid-free paper.

Because of the dynamic nature of the Internet, any web
addresses or links contained in this book may have changed
since publication and may no longer be valid. The views
expressed in this work are solely those of the author and do
not necessarily reflect the views of the publisher, and the
publisher hereby disclaims any responsibility for them.

Contents

Part II

Part III

Part IV

Part V

Part VI

Part VII

Part VIII

Part IX

Introduction

"Obedience Rather Than Sacrifice"

Those who know the scriptures and who
have left the worldly traditions . . .
Will relate to obedience to God and submission.
With the decisions we sometimes have to make,
No matter how hard it is or what it may take.

With an attitude of prayer and belief . . .
It's His will we must seek.
Sometimes we come face to face with our fears,
With the shedding of many tears.

How do we face our fears?
By knowing that God is with us and is always near.
With each step we take,
We live under God's Grace.

He knows our heart . . .
When we're willing to take the first step; then we can start.
It's a day by day decision,
With the Heavenly Father's provision.

My earthly husband,
Is to be the head of the household and is loving.
When I've chosen the wrong path,
He corrects me and when I am quick
to submit, it is God's promise that lasts.

Submitting yourselves one to another in the fear of God . . .
Wive's submit yourselves unto your own
husbands as unto the Lord.
He who is your covering with a blessing in store.
Husband's love your own wive's, even as Christ loves the church.
As husband and wife through prayer we are to search.

Search for God's will in our lives . . .
As the two become one in the presence of Christ.
We submit to His will by submitting to one another.
Because our obedience to God is the example
that is revealed to many others.

Husband's are to love their wive's . . .
Wive's are to respect their husband's for life.
He protects me when I am making a foolish decision,
But most of all he is being a loving husband;
Because God is giving us His promise and His vision.

Obedience rather than sacrifice . . .
When we sacrifice we believe we are doing good in our own eyes.
But it is the obedience to God as husband and wife,
That brings Glory to God's Name as the bride of Christ.

God's plan for a Holy Marriage . . .

"Submitting yourselves one to another in the fear of God . . .
Wives, submit yourselves unto your own husbands, as unto the
Lord . . . For the husband is the head of the wife, even as Christ
is the head of the church: and he is the savior of the body . . .
Therefore as the church is subject unto Christ, so let the wives
be to their own husbands in everything . . . Husbands, love
your wives, even as Christ also loved the church, and gave
himself for it; That he might sanctify and cleanse it with the
washing of water by the word, . . . That he might present it to
himself a glorious church, not having spot, or wrinkle, or any
such thing; but that it should be holy and without blemish . . .
So, ought men to love their wives as their own bodies. He that
loveth his wife loveth himself" . . . Ephesians 6: 21-28 KJV

Part I

Obedience Rather Than Sacrifice

I Samuel 15:22

"Behold, to obey is better than sacrifice" . . .

I have always wanted to write an article on obedience rather than sacrifice. It has taken me many years to understand the concept that submitting to the Lord is far greater than what we can do in sacrificing our lives in thinking we are pleasing our Lord and Savior.

It all began when I moved back in with my parents in 1983 at the age of 31 and lived in their home for five years. I was divorced during that time period for six years. As a teenager I didn't understand the meaning of submitting to my parents: (CHILDREN, obey your parents in the Lord: for this is right. Honor your father and mother, which is the first commandment with promise.) Ephesians 6: 1, 2 KJV

After becoming a Christian in 1983 God created circumstances where I needed to move back in with my father and mother. God prepared me in the school of a Christian life and what it means to be submissive to one's parents at the age of 31. Since I lived in their household I learned about how much my father new in life and his experiences helped lead me to open my eyes in how to submit to them in each circumstance that came along the way.

I remember that I had went to an oral surgeon for my gums when I first moved in with them. The doctor wanted to perform surgery almost right away. He needed a lot of money to perform the surgery. I asked my Dad for the money but instead of him giving the money to me he said, "Why don't you get a second opinion and talk to your sister too?" She, had the same doctor to do the surgery on her. Her gums were in a lot of pain and she needed to wear a mouth guard at night. She, advised me to go for a second opinion and when I did the dentist said, "There was no need for surgery." Continue to brush, dental floss, and have check ups twice a year. Now at this time at the age of 61. I only need a cleaning once a year including brushing and dental flossing everyday. I couldn't praise the Lord enough for saving me from all that pain and money. God is good at all times.

On other occasions there were difficult situations. I could of made a huge mistake by marrying a man who was a con-artist even though he was truly active in the church. After a couple of years of going with him, Dad and Mom were getting ready to move to there home town. Both of them encouraged me not to stay and marry him even though the man said, "He thought it was the Lord's will to get married." It could have been a real mistake. I prayed and sought for godly council from one of Dad's friend's, "He told me that I would know what to do when the time was right." My decision was to move with my parents and start fresh. I had promised God and myself I would never marry again unless I received their blessings. In this case I did not receive it.

So, here I am married to a wonderful husband that I met at a Christian singles after I moved far away with my parents in a different state in 1989. To make a long story short Dad and Mom gave their blessings when my husband, asked me to marry him. It's true I have made some mistakes along the way by not listening to him in certain areas of my life but oh, how I repented. God has been merciful and turned my disobedience out for our good and His glory. There are many times that I have chosen to be submissive to my husband and God has blessed us so, because God says, in: Ephesians 5:22 (Wives, submit yourselves unto your own husbands, as unto the Lord)

"Obedience is Better Than Sacrifice"!!

A Living Sacrifice . . .

To be Crucified with Christ

We who are dead in trespasses and sin . . .
Nothing to gain, nothing to win.
When one comes to the Lord in prayer,
By asking Jesus in faith, He will be there.

He cleansed us by the blood of the Lamb . . .
God gave us a second plan.
To forgive one when we ask Him
with a repentant heart.
He gives one a new beginning, a new start.

By walking in faith with Jesus . . .
As babes in Christ, one takes new
steps as His word feeds us.
It's a continual commitment to our Lord and Savior.
Through trial and error by faith,
we develop a new behavior.

One learns of His love and how He freed us . . .
Through the blood of Jesus.
At the cross through the resurrection
of our Lord Jesus Christ.
One is accepted into His fold and begins a new life.

We witness to each other . . .
In Jesus Christ through the Heavenly Father.
One's body is presented as a living sacrifice,
As one is conformed to the image of Jesus Christ.

Dying to the flesh is what keeps
one alive unto Christ . . .
While in this journey of life.
One becomes a born again believer,
The Lord becomes one's best friend,
and draws one even nearer.

I live but yet not I, it is the Christ
who lives within . . .
All glory, honor and praise belongs to Him,
I present my body as a living sacrifice,
To be crucified with Christ.

I beseech you therefore, brethren, by the mercies of God, that
ye present your bodies a living sacrifice, holy, acceptable
unto God, which is your reasonable service . . . .
Romans 12:1 KJV

Knowing this, that our old man is crucified with Him,
that the body of sin might be destroyed, that henceforth
we should not serve sin . . . Romans 6:6 KJV

Coming Out Of Bondage

Dear Lord, Help our blinded eyes to see . . .
The truth in God's word sets us free.
Open our ears to hear so, we
may enter into Your rest.
Instead of a heart of stone, give us a heart of flesh.

Open our mouth with a shout . . .
Let us believe in our hearts with out a doubt.
That faith comes by hearing God's word.
Work out our salvation with fear
and trembling and in return.

Low and behold, through God's plan . . .
We have the promise of God so, we
may enter the promised land.
In Christ we have the peace of God within.
He, who delivers us from our sin.

The Lord Jesus our Master . . .
Promises us that He will look after.
All the needs of His people.
To be strong in the Lord, not to be feeble.

Let's commit to Jesus our lives . . .
His burden is easy, His load is light.
He is the Lord, who sets the captives free.
So, in the Holy Spirit of God we breathe.

Through the breath of God, let the
Holy Spirit be released . . .
In Jesus Christ we are already made complete.
Let us speak the Word of God in faith.
Let the chains fall from around us
with each step that we take.

Faith, hope, love in God takes us toward freedom . . .
Jesus Christ the Son of God to lean on.
Let go of anything that may bind us.
Be free at last by coming out of bondage.

Dear Lord Jesus, Help Us To Walk The Talk

Dear Lord Jesus,
Help us not only to talk the talk,
But help us to walk the talk.
For those around who may see us.

Look into our hearts, dear Lord,
If there is any wicked or impure
motives within us, we pray.
Give us courage to renounce our worldly ways.
We are your children, help us to go forward.

Give us Your wisdom, help us to obey,
For You are the first and the last.
Let us in You proclaim a fast,
To guide us the rest of the way.

Give us courage not to just talk the talk.
Nor just to put on a good front for others,
But to surrender our lives to the Heavenly Father.
In so doing we will be able to walk the talk.

The Greatest of These is Love . . .

F aith in God.
A ble to lead one in the journey he trods.
I llumanating Christ in one's life.
T hrough God's forgiveness.
H e gives mercy in His presence.

H ope for those who have been told.
O nward toward the mark of the goal.
P rayer that leads one through temptation.
E nduring the test in this life in preparation.

L ove the most important of all three.
O ne with Jesus through one's testimony.
V ictory through the shed blood of Christ.
E ver to live in faith, hope and love in this life.

Faith, Hope, Love and the greatest of these is Love . . .
I Corinthians 13: 13 KJV

Faith to believe . . .
Hope for the lost so, that they might see . . .
Love that covers as the Holy Spirit leads . . .
To total victory . . .

Faithful Is The Lord

Faithful is the Lord . . .
To keep His Holy Word,
Drawing one to Jesus.
So, that He can free us.

Free one from the power of sin and death . . .
A place that one can find God's rest.
Rest for one's soul in a weary land.
All in one accord as one makes his stand.

A stand on God's Word . . .
In hand with God's Sword.
When one is faithful to Jesus the Messiah,
Then He has tried us.

To cleanse one from the blemishes of this life . . .
By the living Word, which is the Christ.
To remain faithful to Him in this world.
By truly being grateful, "For Faithful is the Lord".

God Softens The Blow

When we sometimes feel tossed to and fro . . .
God softens the blow,
When the winds seem treacherous.
Hang on a little longer, for God will bless us.

God did not promise us that we would
not have trials to face . . .
But through each case,
God has a plan to fulfill in us, for His Name's sake.
No matter what it may take.

What trial may you be going through? . . .
The one that keeps nagging at you?
Take heart my friends,
Let's prepare ourselves for the
coming of the noon tide end.

It ends in God's peace for us . . .
All it takes is a little faith and trust.
Find yourself in Christ,
And hold on tight.

It is a fight to the end . . .
For this reason God sent to us all, dear friends,
Jesus the Christ so, that we may know.
God is there for us, to soften the blow.

Grateful To Be Forgiven

Christ, bled and died on the cross . . .
On the first day of the week, He was
resurrected from the dead for the lost.
Yes, I am grateful to be forgiven,
With the price that Jesus paid for
our sin we experience freedom.

Freedom from the power of sin . . .
Satan thought he would win,
As Jesus took His last breath.
Satan, through his hatred failed to foresee the rest.

God's plan for our salvation . . .
The whole world in all creation.
Jesus only asks that we would forgive our fellowman.
Forgive and you shall be forgiven is the plan.

Yes, it is true that we must confess
our sins to Him . . .
And ask Him to cleanse us in the
blood of the Lamb for our sins.
Then to accept His forgiveness
that our Lord Jesus gives,
And to be truly grateful to receive the
gift of salvation, so we may live.

It is a day by day walk . . .
While we learn to listen to the Lord when He talks.
He speaks through His word for all to understand.
Jesus prays that we continue in His love as planned.
When He gives us a new heart . . .
We become pliable in the Masters hand as we start.
Our new journey takes us in a new
direction, that makes life worth living.
Then we find ourselves "Grateful to be Forgiven"

Healing Words for a Hurting Heart

Disappointed by mankind . . .
Healing words that come in time.
Remembering that we are sinners from the start.
Painful words that create a hurting heart.

Help us Lord to remember where we come from . . .
That we are a work in progress until
our work here on earth is done.
You forgave a sinner like me,
Help me to forgive those who
have hurt me is my plea.

Only, Jesus can heal us with His words . . .
Words of comfort from our Lord.
He forgives those who ask Him to
through His shed blood.
Let go and let God have His way with
each one, through His Son.

When Jesus took our place on Calvary
and pleaded for me and you . . .
He prayed, "Father forgive them for
they know not what they do."
If you have wounds that can not heal.
Take it to the One who knows how you feel.

Healing Words . . .
Come from God's word so, one can go forward.
Hurting heart . . .
Pray for God's forgiveness and a fresh start.

A new day begins through Him, a new start . . .
With healing words for a hurting heart.
"Forgive and ye shall be forgiven."
The only stipulation in God's word that was given.

Don't point a finger . . .
In prayer, let one linger.
Pray for God's forgiveness for you
and the one who hurts.
Healing words for a hurting heart.

Jesus The Giver Of Life

Jesus the giver of life . . .
No one could imagine what would be His plight.
Appointed by God, to give His only
begotten Son on the cross.
A decision Jesus made out of love for the lost.

Jesus loves His Father more than anything . . .
He laid down His life willingly.
How could Jesus take the pain and humiliation?
Because He looked upon us as a
broken and fallen creation.

God loves each one of us . . .
He desires our love and our trust.
God is pure and holy, this is how He
created us from the start.
He created us in His image and set us apart.

God wanted us to return His love . . .
By surrendering our will to the
Heavenly Father above.
We have a choice in this life.
Whom do we choose to serve today, will it be Christ?

We make decisions everyday . . .
When we kneel before the Lord and pray.
Let us come humbly before His throne.
Cleanse us Lord and let Your blood atone.

For without You . . .
We would perish tis true.
Thank you, dear Lord for taking our place,
And allowing us to live under Your grace.

Just Because

Jesus died, Just Because . . .
Of His unconditional love for the lost.
Just because we sinned, He did
not count it as a total loss.
A second plan, God thought.

God's only begotten Son was nailed to the cross . . .
Christ was risen from the dead, the real cause.
Showing us all,
His love for us is true, never false.

Jesus came to this world and brought . . .
Life, no longer to live under the law.
Through God's love, He sought,
To save us from the fall.

Listen to the Savior's gentle call . . .
The truth is a powerful tool because,
Jesus gives us liberty and freedom in our thoughts.
To worship and adore Jesus, Just Because.

The Just Shall Live By Faith

By Living Under God's Grace

Faith, the substance of things hoped for . . .
And the evidence of things not seen.
Faith in action when we praise the Lord.
Spiritual blessings for each one to receive.

Jesus going before us . . .
To lead the way.
Directed by God's word for the just.
Being directed by the Holy Spirit when one prays.

Each day there is much to rejoice in . . .
Because our home awaits us with Jesus in heaven.
Knowing that we belong to Jesus as our best friend.
Jesus taught the disciples of faith through
His grace, the chosen eleven.

If, taken one day at a time . . .
He, who has faith in God to believe.
Then his candle stick will not be
hidden but will shine.
So, that one may with gladness receive.

Receive prayers that are answered . . .
By letting God have His way.
With rejoicing and a shout before
the Lord with dancing.
God is able to remove the mountain when one prays.

Set free from all worry . . .
"The just shall live by faith."
Knowing God is Holy,
By living under God's grace.

Make Our Hearts Pliable In Your Hands

When our hearts are tried . . .
Let us begin to apply.
God's Word in our hearts,
Then we are able to start.

Start, by listening to God's Word . . .
For by His word we have heard.
The gospel of Christ made simple to us,
Then He is able to protect.

Protect, us from the enemies snares . . .
So, we do not give up in despair.
As God continues to help us prepare,
And makes it possible for Him to care.

Care, for us in the way He chooses to . . .
He chooses life for me and you,
Through the blood of Jesus Christ.
He died on the cross, willing to sacrifice His life.

He gives us a choice to decide if
we will serve Christ . . .
No longer through our own might.
For each of our lives, You have a plan,
By helping make our hearts pliable in Your hands.

Only, If My People Would Pray . . .

"If my people who are called by My Name"
"Will humble themselves and pray"
Their lives would never be the same.
"By putting off the old man and
putting on the new"
In this way.

"And seek My Face"
They would live under God's grace.
"And turn from their wicked ways"
Each thought being cleansed by the blood,
Then God would say;

"Then I will hear from heaven"
"I will forgive their sins"
So, Christ can begin,
"And heal our land"
When we take that first step and make our stand.

Only, if my people would pray . . .

My prayer is . . .
Dear Heavenly Father,
Teach us how to pray and what to ask for . . .
Open our spiritual eyes and ears to Your truth . . .
Help us to be bold in the Lord . . .
And help us not to be self righteous . . .
But righteous by choosing what
is right in God's eyes . . .

"Seek ye first the kingdom of God
and His righteousness"
Thank you Lord for Your Word . . .
Who came in the flesh through Jesus Christ . . .
For He is the Word . . .
He is the Beginning and the End . . .
Alpha and Omega . . .
From A to Z . . .
Thank you, for hearing our prayers . . .
For without You we are nothing and
can do nothing of ourselves . . .
Give all glory, honor and praise
to Jesus Christ Name . . .
Amen!!!

If my people who are called by my Name will humble themselves and pray and seek my face and turn from their wicked ways . . . Then will I hear from Heaven, forgive their sins and heal their land . . . II Chronicles 7:14 KJV

Peace . . . Knowing We Are Forgiven

We find no peace in this world . . .
Or in our worldly goods.
They are but like the grass,
Worldly goods do not last.

Yes, they may give you a feel good emotion . . .
But is only a token,
Of a broken life,
A false crutch for the moment,
in place of the Christ.

How does one find true peace? . . .
Jesus stands through the storms
of life never to cease.
He is our foundation of our salvation.
It is simple you see, first confess your sin to Him.

Cleansed by the blood of the Lamb . . .
It was all in God's plan,
The perfect sacrifice,
The One who paid the ultimate price.

Jesus the Son of God was not afraid . . .
But prayed,
For God's will to be done.
For Jesus was the perfect sacrifice,
the only Begotten Son.

Where does the peace of God come from? . . .
From Jesus Christ, God's Son.
Knowing He took our place,
And did it for our sake.

This is a reassurance that we find
peace in knowing . . .
That Christ forgave you and me by showing,
How much He wants us to be His own.
Never again to be alone.

It is a peace that the world does not have for us . . .
Let's put our faith and trust.
In Jesus Christ and live life,
To the fullest in Christ.

Jesus leaves with us His peace . . .
The enemy of the flesh, world
and Satan He did defeat.
The day Christ was resurrected from the cross.
With faith in our Jesus, never more to be lost.

Peace in knowing we are forgiven . . .
Of all our sins, makes life worth living.
The unconditional love of Christ, He has given.
Brings us peace, in knowing we are forgiven.

And the peace of God, which passeth all
understanding shall keep your hearts and minds
through Christ Jesus . . . Phillippians 4:7 KJV

Rest In Christ Jesus

Let us find rest in Christ Jesus . . .
It is in Him only that we can be blessed.
No such thing as luck, I do not jest.
Only, do we find God's favor on us.

Let us find rest for the weary soul . . .
Quench our thirst Lord, through the living word.
Help us to find the peace you give so, freely.
Ask for God's unconditional love and mercy.

Jesus Christ the Master of all things . . .
In control of the universe in His Holy Name.
Prince of peace.
All things placed under His feet.

Ask and it will be given unto you . . .
Seek and you will find God's truth.
Trust the Almighty God for all things in this life.
Let there be joy and laughter in
our hearts instead of strife.

Let God have His way . . .
Then we can say.
With God's reassurance,
By giving us the faith to find rest in Christ Jesus.

Rest In The Lord

Let us take time out to regroup . . .
When we have been in the front lines
for awhile, help us Lord to cope.
Cope with the fact that it is okay to find
the time just by being with You.
Our bodies and spirit need to take
time out to see things through.

We are human . . .
When God hits the enemy hard through God's Son.
Then to us what seems like defeat,
The enemy with his devices hits us
hard when we feel weak.

But God is faithful . . .
For this I am truly grateful.
So, when wounded in the battle field,
Put back on your armor as a shield.

Satan that old deceiver . . .
Wants us to believe he has won the
victory instead of Jesus.
He is a liar from the start,
In Christ we have the blood of
Jesus to cover our hearts.

Don't listen to him . . .
The enemy likes for us to think of
him as the one who wins.
In reality Jesus has already won from before,
So, let us take time to be with Jesus
to find Rest in the Lord.

Reverence And Obedience In Jesus

Jesus came into this world to serve . . .
Jesus has a servants heart, one that deserves,
Reverence and Obedience
In Jesus.

Jesus humbled Himself before
His Father in heaven . . .
And expressed what is required of
us through His chosen eleven.
By washing the disciples feet along with Peter's,
Jesus set the example for us as our
humble Savior and leader.

He showed us who God truly is . . .
A God of love who is always in our mist.
Ask Jesus anything according to His
will and He will do it for you.
God receives the glory and you will
receive His joy through and through.

When we take Jesus at His word . . .
As we become mature and go forward.
As our Heavenly Father, He too desires to please us.
Let us reverence Him through
our obedience in Jesus.

The Church

(A Prayer, Dear Lord)

Dear Lord, we send up an S.O.S . . .
Our churches are in distress.
The Holy Spirit is not able to move,
We've gotten away from God's absolutes and truths.

We think up of man made ways
to solve our problems . . .
Our self sufficiency is rooted in our sin of cobwebs.
The sin of wanting more in numbers,
While the church sleeps and slumbers.

Dear Lord, forgive us in this nation . . .
For trusting in our own innovations.
We pray Lord for You to move upon the waters.
We kneel before the throne of God's alter.

Help!!!
Let us put away the life of self.
Crucified with Christ, You have broken man's curse.
Thy will be done in earth . . .
As it is in heaven in the church . . .

I do not speak concerning the true church of
Christ but there are some that use man made
alternatives to make it look like things are led
by God . . . God help our churches to come back
to the simple teachings of Jesus Christ . . .

The Commandments of the

Lord are not Grievous

Listen one and all . . .
Listen to the Holy Spirits call.
Jesus speaks of His love for us,
Through His Word we trust.

It is clear to see . . .
That we have a choice to believe.
In the Great I Am,
We choose to make our stand.

In this land of the free . . .
We have our freedom to believe.
One day this fact may not stand true.
For the red, white and blue.

God please, help us to choose Your ways . . .
As we face each new day.
God has given us His commandments.
So, we may experience His joy of contentment.

Let us forsake the old man . . .
And fulfill God's plan.
Jesus desire for us is to rejoice always,
In whatever circumstance we may
face by doing it God's way.

We cannot please Jesus . . .
Without faith through works as
the Holy Spirit leads us.
Ask Him to purify your intentions,
Because intentions can be pretentious.

His desire for us is to win the race . . .
But it is impossible if we do not place,
Our faith in the Lord Jesus.
He takes our heavy load and sees us.

In a state of ruins as we grope and stumble . . .
Through our own sin we fumble.
We need God's absolutes to keep
us on track to free us,
Because the commandments of
the Lord are not grievous.

The Gift

Let us receive God's gift to us . . .
With a grateful heart through trust.
When Jesus was sent to redeem those,
Who desire with all their hearts to know.

To know God's Son through His love . . .
The mercy He has given us directly
from the Heavenly Father above.
May we remember that God sacrificed the One,
He sent to us to take our place
through Jesus Christ, God's Son.

He was sent as an atonement for our sins,
through Jesus Christ own blood . . .
He dwelt among us, to finish the
work He had begun.
Jesus is pure of heart, the only one
who could possibly take our place.
While dying on the cross, who
knew what it would take?

It took an obedient heart . . .
One who chose to give His life from the start.
A life that was without sin, one
who is pure and holy.
God gave us "the gift" of His Son,
may He receive all glory.

Watch And Pray

Watch and Pray . . .
Through each new day.
The enemy seeks one to devour.
Help us Lord, to be faithful in prayer
even for just one hour.

Yes, our flesh is weak . . .
The enemy will do everything to keep.
Our minds busy and doing all kinds of things.
Distractions in playing his game.

It's true with every Christian . . .
That knows our Lord Jesus, when
we seek His wisdom.
The wisdom that is not of this world
Is to give reverence to Jesus our Lord.

Yes, watch and pray . . .
So, we may overcome all temptations in this way.
We have victory through the blood of Christ.
The devil has no power over our lives.

When we watch and pray . . .
Trust our Lord Jesus in what to say.
He knows our hearts,
His children are set apart.

A peculiar people . . .
To stand strong in God's word, no longer feeble.
A prayer warrior that believes in what God says,
While we His people "Watch and Pray"

When The Enemy Condemns,
Our Jesus Will Defend

"Let us Rejoice in Jesus and Praise Him"

Let me take a little time to reflect . . .
I know Jesus is here to protect.
He protects His children in the wilderness of life.
God promises us that He has forgiven us through the
Blood Of Christ.

Yet, as His children we often spend
time by being afraid . . .
We are sometimes afraid of missing
the mark if we are not brave.
One of the enemies greatest tools against
God's children is to condemn them,
But it is Jesus job to defend the
weakest of His children in Him.

Jesus has a plan . . .
He wants His children to be able to stand,
Stand against the wiles of the enemy.
So, that His children can be set free.

Let us take our mind off of ourselves . . .
So, we may praise and worship God, then dwell.
Dwell on our Heavenly Father, through
Jesus where there is love and trust.
Out of the enemy's condemnation that binds us.

Help us Lord to focus . . .
Focus on You, for You Lord have chosen us.
Let us put on the whole Amour of
God and stand our ground.
With a two edged sword in our hand and
the praises of God in our mouth,
proclaiming the Christ whom we have found.

When the enemy condemns . . .
Our Jesus is there to defend.
Jesus, defends us from the enemy's accusations.
Let us Rejoice in Jesus and Praise Him.

Who is he that condemneth? It is Christ that died, yea rather,
that is risen again, who is even at the right hand of God,
who also maketh intercession for us. Romans 8:34 KJV

Whom The Lord Has Set Free Is Free Indeed

There are two kinds of freedom to be considered . . .
To begin with this is not a riddle.
There is the kind the world counts as being free.
If it feels good, do it, this is their philosophy.

The carnal man . . .
Cannot understand.
Their eyes are blind they cannot see,
What it truly means to be free.

Free from sin and death . . .
That manifests itself in the flesh.
We cannot be set free without the blood of Christ,
As our pure and sinless sacrifice.

True freedom comes from knowing the Lord . . .
And realizing what He has in store.
We may experience pain and sorrow,
But God promises us a new tomorrow.

One without the guilt of our sins . . .
Then to be cleansed.
From all our past, present and future sins,
When we've made the decision to repent.

No need to look back in our past . . .
Enjoy His presence in the present.
The future remains in His providence,
This is His freedom that we experience.
For Whom the Lord sets free is free indeed . . .

A Prayer of Adoration

Dear Jesus . . .
Please, forgive us.
Forgive us of our sin,
So, that we may enter in.

Enter into Your Gate . . .
With Praise.
From dusk until dawn,
Let us praise you all day long.

Sing praises to the King of kings . . .
Our offerings we bring.
Into Your court,
To Christ our Lord.

Thank you for Your sacrifice . . .
By giving Your life.
Upon the cross You did die,
Being raised from the dead was Your plight.

How we worship and adore, our Lord . . .
Thanking You, for the blessings in store.
Now we have peace and rest,
As He takes us through each trial and test.

Buried with Christ Jesus . . .
We are risen with Him through crucifying the flesh.
Trust in Him for all things,
While we praise and sing.
Hallelujah . . .
Hallelujah . . .
Praise His Holy Name.
For it is from God, Jesus came.
King of kings . . .
Lord of lords . . .
We kneel down before,
It is You, who we worship and adore.

As our Father . . .
We bring honor,
To Your Name,
The gospel of Christ we proclaim.

Everyday Remains A Blessing

Everyday is a gift from God,
Look to Jesus in this world we trod.
Facing new challenges,
Jesus takes one's life then balances it.

He takes away the old and gives us the new.
A new way of thinking as we walk through,
The trials and the cares of this life.
Jesus stands in the gap for us,
the one they call Christ.

Without Jesus we would be nothing,
It's because of Him that we have faith in trusting.
Trusting the one and only Jesus Christ.
It is a privilege to be a part of His life.

In the daily walk with the Lord.
He gives us our daily bread with His word.
His Holy Spirit convicts us when we sin,
So, we have an advocate with the
Father and ask Him to cleanse.

Cleanse me dear Lord of my sins,
Purify my thoughts and sanctify me through Him.
Wash me white as snow,
So, the Lord Jesus I may know.

Through Jesus I can rejoice in Him,
I find peace of mind and contentment within.
I cannot praise Jesus the Son God enough.
Even when life seems tough . . .

For I find in Him that "Everyday
Remains a Blessing"
Through trials and temptations.
Through failures and setbacks.
I count it a joy in knowing Jesus,
no longer to turn back.

Jesus cleanses me with the blood of the Lamb,
To be His child forever I am.
Free in sharing the gospel of Christ for His glory.
Everyday remains a blessing
through the gospels story.

Reaping The Harvest

The harvest truly is plentiful . . .
Many seek to fill their empty souls.
Empty inside,
Is there someone to answer their cry?

A cry for help . . .
To be delivered from sin and self.
Is there more to life,
Than meets the eye?

What is the answer, does anyone know?
Dear Jesus, lead the way and show.
Show us the way we should go,
No longer to be tossed about to and fro.

We as the church . . .
Lord, give us a heart to search.
Searching to redeem the time,
Salted with the seasoning of Jesus Christ.

Let our light so shine . . .
In a world that Satan blinds.
The Sewer plants the seeds of life,
They are watered by our Lord Jesus Christ.

Go tell it on the mountain . . .
That there is a fountain.
Where we will thirst no more,
Clear waters that gently flow.

From the living waters of the Holy Spirit . . .
We will thirst no more because
of Jesus who was pierced.
Pierced in His side, for all mankind.
Jesus who freely laid down His life.

He saw what it would be like with
a life without Him . . .
Doomed to a life to die in our sins.
When mankind sinned he lost his first state and fell,
We were doomed for an eternal life in hell.

Dear Lord, let us remain faithful to Your calling . . .
By planting seeds of Your Word in
hearts who are wondering.
Wondering if there is anything
more to this life at best?
While we plant His seeds, Jesus will
be Reaping the Harvest.

Part II

A Prayer of Thanksgiving

In the first few months of our marriage I was learning to be submissive to my husband in different areas of my life. He had been married before and had lost his wife to diabetes. It was extremely hard on him for the first two years.

After a few months of being married we moved into his previous home they owned. I realized it would be a hard transition for him by letting go of certain things and I understood there were still lots of wonderful memories he still wanted to hang on to.

She and I had different tastes with decor and furnishings. I wanted to change a few things at first but I had a lot to learn. I wanted to get a new couch among other things but we weren't in a financial position where we could just go out and buy what we wanted. My husband said, let's wait.

I got the idea that I could go out and buy a couch cover. He didn't really like the idea of covering it up. I said, okay Lord, I want to please my husband and I thanked the Lord for the way things were. I eventually forgot about the incident. I had no idea what God was going to allow next in our lives that would change our whole situation.

We went on a visit to his mom's for a couple of days. We enjoyed the scenery and the beauty of the flat lands on the way home.

We pulled up to the house and we could not believe what we were seeing. In disbelief we drove around the block and then just sat there in front of our house looking at it. It had been all boarded up. How could this of happened? In a state of shock we pulled into the driveway and couldn't believe our eyes.

About that time our neighbor next door came over and filled us in. He said, "Someone had ran into our house with a one ton truck." It came from on top of the hill down through our yard, past the tree and right smack dab into the living room window. Our neighbor had been kind enough to stay at our house before they came to board it up so, no one would vandalize it.

After getting over our disbelief, our shock of hearing the story, we couldn't believe it was true. Although our response was all together different in the situation than I could have ever imagined. We were calm about it and thought to ourselves God must have a plan. At a different time in our lives our reaction would be to sizzle with anger. It's amazing how God takes one's life and can mold it like the clay on the spindle.

We entered into the house, there was glass everywhere. His grandmothers library table was turned upside down. We went into the master bedroom and the door trap had bounced off the hallway ceiling onto our bedroom floor. I could just imagine the impact it had on the house. You must be wondering how could something like this turn into something good?

The next day our insurance man had men working on putting everything back together. They cleaned up all the debris and replaced the window in one day. Things moved along and in time there was the fun of shopping for new items. Paint for the living room, new curtains, a new living room rug.

They redid his grandmothers library table and brought back all it's lustrous beauty, last but not least a beautiful new couch. I couldn't believe the way the Lord had answered my prayer of thanksgiving.

A true story of events. I Thessalonians 5:18

A New Day

Dear Lord,
As I take time to pray . . .
I just want to say,
I love you more each new day.

You are my everything . . .
I just want to sing,
Of Your goodness and love.
What You have given from above.

You sent Your Son, Christ . . .
Satan didn't give up without a fight.
Jesus hung on the cross and took our place.
He did it out of unconditional love for our sake.

With Jesus on the right hand of Heaven's Throne . . .
God made it possible so, we could belong.
When we repent, acknowledge Christ
and ask for forgiveness,
Then we are adopted into the family
of God under His grace.

Thank you Lord for Your mercy on us . . .
We were lost and You found away to give trust.
Jesus is the Savior of our souls,
He is the foundation to our Salvation.

With a new day at hand . . .
It is on God's word I stand.
Bring us back to the absolutes in life,
What is right in God's sight.

Help us to remember it is because of You . . .
That we can be grateful too.
With each new day to approach our goal,
To be more like our Father, whom we adore.

The challenge . . .
That God gives us a balance.
In our lives while we pray,
By giving God the glory for "A New Day"

A Walk With You

A walk in the woods . . .
The sun shines through the tree leaves . . .
Enjoying my time with you . . .

The Tanka Poem

Dishes in the sink
Laundry left in the dryer
Look at where I am.
Writing because I love to,
Share God's love with everyone.

Abba . . . Father

Our fathers here on earth . . .
Try to give good gifts of worth.
But if we ask Jesus,
How much more He will give us.

Our fathers sometimes fail . . .
It's not for lack of love, humans can be frail.
It is just that we are human in this world,
Our Father gives us His love
through these empty shells.

We as His children . . .
Desire to please, our Father in heaven.
Jesus gives us a new heart,
One that can say, I love You, Lord, with pure delight.

Some may not have a Father . . .
But there is none other.
That is like Jesus, as our,
Abba . . . Father

A . . . S . . . K

Ask and it shall be given unto you . . .
Jesus is faithful and true.
He waits for us to come to Him
Ask—forgiveness through Christ for sin.

Seek and you shall find . . .
our living Savior while there is time.
His Kingdom is not of this world
Seek eternity—find it in the Lord.

Knock and it shall be opened unto you . . .
God will show you what to do.
Trust in His word for it is true
Knock—Christ is the Door and waits for you.

Matthew 7: 7-8

By: Cinda M Carter and Tom Blakely

All Things Become New

When under the shadow of His wings . . .
Protected through Jesus our King.
Without even realizing He is there,
God shows His goodness to all
mankind while we are here.

Jesus draws us near . . .
He uses our circumstances, even our fears.
The Lord knows we are a lost human race,
So, God sent Jesus to give us His grace.

When we realize that we are in need of a Savior . . .
To fill our void hearts with a love that is greater.
Greater than anyone can imagine or ask for,
No one could fill that void in our
hearts but the Master.

When we accept Jesus as Lord in our lives . . .
Our sins are cleansed by the blood of Jesus Christ.
He brings us into His fold,
No longer to be under the grasp of the enemies hold.

We become babes in Jesus Christ . . .
Through His word, Jesus starts
planting the seeds of life.
How could I have not seen this
before says, the believer,
I was under Satan's influence, the
prince of darkness, that deceiver.

Now into God's word I find myself
being nourished . . .
No longer under the curse to perish.
It's because of Jesus that I can bask in His love,
Sent by our Heavenly Father above.

No longer living in the flesh . . .
But by the Spirit of God instead of death.
The old life is dead,
No longer to raise its ugly head.

Through Jesus the old life is crucified with Christ . . .
By faith in my Lord and Savior there is a new life.
All things are possible with God,
it is for us to choose.
When we choose Jesus, the old life is
proclaimed dead, then made new.

"All Things Become New"

Therefore we are buried with Him by baptism into death; that like as Christ was raised up from the dead by the glory of the Father, even so we also should walk in newness of life . . . For if we have been planted together in the likeness of His death, we shall be also in the likeness of His resurrection . . . Romans 6:4-5 KJV

Part III

The Night of the Delivery

In the first week of May 1991, my daughter was due to have her baby. My husband and I decided it was time to make a trip down to Tulsa, Oklahoma where my daughter and her husband lived at the time. Our trip took around nine hours to drive. We had no idea what was going to take place while we were in for our visit. We had planned just staying a day or two at the most.

I was hoping and praying that the baby would be born during the time we were visiting but what are the chances of that happening? Slim to almost none but God had a plan.

We had the baby shower the first day we arrived. We fixed up the room for the homecoming, not realizing when the baby would be born or what it was going to be. There was excitement in the air. We were preparing for a new life to come into this world. We hung curtains, put the bassinet up and set everything in place.

That same night my daughter's water bag broke. We all moved into action. There were a few people that came in while we were still at my daughter's house. They all loaded up in their car, five adults including my daughter, her husband and baby made six. My husband and I followed them on the way to the hospital. It was pouring down rain in the wee hours of the morning.

Then we heard this thumping, repeatedly. Thump, Thump, Thump! We saw them pulling off to the side of the highway. Hon, "what are they doing?" He said "I think they have a flat tire." At that point they all jumped out of the car and were coming toward us. By God's grace somehow they all fit into the car. One by one they got into the car with my husband driving, me in the middle and another person in the front seat with us. My daughter and her husband with the others climbed into the back seat. I counted heads and their were seven of us in one car and baby made eight. We moved on as they gave us directions in which way to take. The first hospital wouldn't take them since she was only dilated three centimeters. So, we moved on and was in search for another hospital. By the time we arrived at the next one she was dilated five centimeters then, admitted into the hospital.

My husband, as the grandfather to be, two grandmothers, cousins and friends were their that night to see the baby delivered. Only two or three were allowed in the delivery room. While we were waiting outside and she was in labor, I decided I was going to move a chair in place in the waiting room to sit down. About that time, believe it or not my back went out. I couldn't believe it. I made my way to the emergency room to be checked out by a doctor. It was quite await and I could hardly wait to get back upstairs before the baby was born. They gave me some muscle relaxers to help with the pain. Eventually I made my way back upstairs.

I really don't remember at what time the baby was born but I do remember how I felt when I held my new baby granddaughter in my arms for the first time. It was simply amazing how God had worked the whole thing out for us to be there to make sure my daughter and everyone got to the hospital safely and on time.

God's timing is always perfect, he is never late. Jesus is always on time for us in whatever situation we may find ourselves in. Who would of guessed it would be split second timing. A new baby girl was born into this world. Then to be able to be apart of it was so, amazing. God will never cease to amaze me.

A Friend Loves At All Times

In Jesus I find . . .
One who is faithful and kind.
A friend loves at all times.

He is one you can trust . . .
There is no other like Jesus.
A friend loves at all times.

A friend that sticks closer than a brother . . .
We need not look any further.
A friend loves at all times.

What must we do? . . .
To be accepted into His fold for me and you?
Jesus forgives when we ask Him to.

Then He claims us as His own . . .
Because He has shown.
A Friend loves at all times.

Proverbs 17:17
Proverbs 18:24

Be Still My Soul

Be still my soul
As Jesus unfolds.
The mystery Of His secrets,
Through His Word and the Holy Spirit.

While meditating in His Word.
I will listen to the Lord.
For there are found treasures,
Of a lasting kind forever.

He will draw nigh, when He hears us cry.
It pleases the Lord to hear our replies.
The fact that we call on the Master.
In silence Jesus will bring us joy and laughter.

Help, me to be bold.
To speak of Your love to be told.
Help me to speak the truth in love,
Centered on Christ above.

I will focus on Jesus,
He is the one who frees us.
Pressing toward the mark of the goal.
Be still my soul.

Begin By Praising Him

Forgiveness . . .
God forgives and has mercy on us.
Take it to the Lord;
Be in agreement with Him in one accord.

If you have sinned against your brother . . .
Drop what your doing; confess
your fault to one another.
Repent and make amends,
To the one who you did offend.

Then take it back to Jesus Christ . . .
For He is the only one who can make it right.
Ask for His forgiveness;
When we come before Him, with a
humble spirit, He will forgive us.

His word promises He will forgive . . .
And cleanse us through His blood from all sin.
With a new beginning through being cleansed,
"Begin by Praising Him".

Christ Death and Resurrection

During Christ death . . .
On the cross He felt separated from His
Father and was deeply perplexed.
Jesus took our sins on Himself and gave His
all while He was being put to the test.
Jesus made it possible for each of
us to enter into His rest.

Christ rose and was resurrected . . .
Our lives and souls were left under His protection.
Even at the last He only thought of others,
He knew that we would be adopted into
God's family as His sisters and brothers.

While Jesus was there dying on the cross . . .
He turned to God and prayed for
a dying world that was lost.
He asked, "Father forgive them for
they know not what they do."
Jesus shed His last drop of blood for me and you.

Jesus would rise again on the third day . . .
Through God's plan of salvation,
Jesus Christ paved the way.
Jesus death was never considered to be an ending.
Because of His death on the cross, it would
be a whole new start, a new beginning.

It was a new beginning for all of mankind . . .
Jesus resurrection would open the eyes of the blind.
It was a humiliating death for all to see on Calvary.
All of those who have faith in Jesus are
cleansed by the blood to be made free.

The devil didn't see God's perfect
plan for our salvation . . .
Satan didn't realize God's plan
through His resurrection.
No greater love than this was ever shown.
Now Jesus sets with God the Father in
His rightful place on the throne.

Now the work is complete in Jesus . . .
We ask You, Lord for Your mercy and forgiveness.
Cleanse us with the blood of the lamb.
So, we too may share salvation's plan.

Thank you, Lord for Your "Only Begotten Son".
Through Your love for us the work was
finished and has only just begun.
It was God's perfect plan for our salvation.
Through "Christ death and resurrection"

Part IV

Mother's Unconditional Love

It was in the year of August 2006. I had just accepted a job for cleaning apartments at a Seniors Assistant Care Home. Thinking I would never to be able to see my mother again because of my schedule at work, God saw what was to come.

Mom and I were not always on the best of terms. I had never really developed a relationship with her through the years because of decisions I had made concerning my marriage when I was young. While raising my daughter, her and I would always bump heads. She had raised us girls and did her very best. Mom was a stay at home mom. Our family was not a perfect one but there was always the feeling of knowing that we were loved.

Dad went on to be with the Lord in February of 1998 at the age of 72 and mom was left alone to make it on her own. My sisters and I filled in on certain occasions and made trips in to help Mom, either going to the doctor, grocery shopping, cleaning and fixing things around the house. We had some good years with mom that followed after Dad's death.

I was terrified of loosing my mother before amends could be made between the two of us. We had some contention that went on for years, there seemed to be no relief in sight. For years I prayed that God would heal the situation between us.

While I was a teenager, just getting out of High School, mom became involved in horoscopes and had us girls involved as well. I too, became overly involved with it, more so, than my sisters. During that time because of unforeseen events that came about, mom had a breakdown. Dad stopped her from reading the books and threw them all away.

Mom was keeping the family together in the forefront for years. Dad had a week-end drinking problem and it just became to much for mom with all that she had on her shoulders. She put her whole heart into our lives and kept us together as a family without us girls even realizing it. Mom helped us with our homework on a regular basis, cooked, cleaned, washed clothes, hung them out on the line and tried to keep us going, even dad in her own way.

It wasn't until the breakdown that Dad and Mom turned their lives over to the Lord.

Dad said, "He would never drink again and he didn't."

Mom committed her life to Jesus and us girls accepted the Lord.

Even though the Lord had been working in their lives, I still was in conflict with myself. I left home and got married a year later after graduation. I guess you could say, I was running from the situation at home. In my marriage of eleven years, I became very self centered and I had a lot to learn before the Lord took hold of my life. Which wasn't until 1983. At the age of thirty-one I moved back in with Mom and Dad, I really had no place else to go. At that point some of the healing process began between my parents and myself. I lived with them for five years. I met my husband in February 1989, then married him in May of 1990.

Back to the beginning of my story on why my job was so, vital to the situation.

The first thing in the morning the girls at work would get together and read horoscopes to see what they were. I would spend time with them without really being involved. The Holy Spirit convicted me in such away, while I still continued to be a part of it. I decided not to join them anymore and prepared for the days work. As time went on, one of the girls started ridiculing me in seductive ways. It was in away that the other girls did not realize that she was directing the comments toward me personally. I made a personal stand in the Lord not to follow the crowd, it was a blow to the enemies plan.

During this time, mom was dying. I just couldn't accept it. I happened to watch a movie at this time about the Dilley Family having sextuplets, who refused to have an abortion in order to save the others. The babies were born on May 25, 1993 but one of the babies was left in the hospital. The mother-in-law thought they should take the crib down until the baby came home. When the father came in and saw that the crib was gone, in faith he claimed it was going back up until the child came home. After a few months the child returned to it's home with the happy family.

How did this movie help me? By taking action! I had bought a hospital bed at a garage sale thinking we may need it someday. Unfortunately, my husband didn't think it would fit in the spare bedroom. I begged to differ. So, while he was at work I went down to the basement and was determined to bring the mattress up the stairs on my own into the bedroom as an act of faith believing mom would live. The hard part was getting the bed itself out of the basement door to the front door. I prayed, Dear Lord, "Please help me." I noticed the neighbor next door and I called out to him. It was still dark outside and I was wondering if he would even see me or hear me. He heard my cry, then came over. We carried the bed around the other side of house and through the front door to put it in our small bedroom. It fit perfectly. On my part it was an act of faith believing mom, would eventually get to come to our house so, we could take care of her. I continued to fix up the bedroom with family pictures and added a feminine touch to the room while I waited on the Lord. I guess you could call it faith in action. This is what I determined in my heart.

On February 19, 2007, it would have been Dad's 82nd birthday. I was talking to mom on the phone. At that point she was close to death.

I said, "Please Mom, I need you, don't go; Please, Mom I need you."

She replied, "I need you too."

I said, "Really, Mom?" I was so, pleased to hear her response.

I told her that I would quit my job. On Dad's birthday I had decided to quit. I needed my mother. The curse had been broken, the fear of loosing my mother and because of the reason I left my family the first time had been resolved.

They flew her in a helicopter over to the Evansville Hospital and the doctor's put in a pacemaker. With time, Mom got better. In March 2007, she came to live with us and was able to stay a year and a half until September of 2008. I now have such good memories to reflect upon.

There were times I would say, harsh words. In so doing, she would assure me that no matter what I said, or did, it would not change her love for me. Mom showed me unconditional love. She was a real trooper. Mom loved her family and told me that I did not realize what I had in my husband. Mom helped save our marriage with good advice. My daughter and our relationship was healed between the two of us.

I cooked for Mom, she was able to get off her insulin nine months within the time span that she stayed with us. We laughed together, we sang, we danced, we held each other, we forgave one another. No one can take away your memories. It was ordained by God. Everything that took place, He worked out for our good and His glory.

My husband and I were no longer able to take care of mom, it was then that she went to live with my sister up north after loosing her husband of 25 years. Mom's death was a painful one and I would talk on the phone with her on a regular basis. I remember the last words she spoke to me, Mom new she was dying and she said, "I love you" in a weak, low sounding voice. I replied, "I love you, Mom."

I remember praying the day before she died and asking, please Lord, don't let her suffer anymore. The next day she went home to be with the Lord, in August of 2010. I cannot praise, God enough for giving me borrowed time with my mom on this earth. She meant so, much to so, many different people. Mom had a fight about her and never gave up on family or friends. Even, now with tears streaming down my face, I will always remember my "Mother's Unconditional Love."

Psalm 119: 153, 154, 157, 173, 174, 175 KJV

153: Consider my affliction, and deliver me: for I do not forget thy law.
154: Plead my cause and deliver me: quicken me according to thy word.
157: Many are my persecutors and mine enemies; yet do I not decline from thy testimonies.
173: Let thine hand help me; for I have chosen thy precepts.
174: I have longed for thy salvation, O Lord; and thy law is my delight.
175: Let my soul live, and it shall praise thee; and let thy judgments help me.
176: I have gone astray like a lost sheep; seek thy servant; for I do not forget thy commandments.

"Mother's Love"

M other we honor her . . .
O vercomer in trials and tribulations,
T ruthful for she keeps her word and her obligations.
H elpful to all that needs a helping hand,
E verlasting love through time that stands.
R ighteousness of Christ,
S elfless from start to finish through her life.

L ove that is enduring . . .
O nly with her love, she's always reassuring.
V isits the lonely whenever she can,
E ternally blessed, with Jesus love she stands.

Dear Lord, Give Me Wisdom

Dear Lord, Give me wisdom . . .
In making my decisions.
Help remind me to pray,
To think about what I am going to say.

Sometimes without thinking I
jump in with both feet . . .
Only because I did not pray and think.
I didn't think of the consequences it would bring.
I was eager to serve without Your leading.

You are truly merciful and You do forgive . . .
Though the damage is done You will bring;
What Satan meant for evil, and
turn it around for good.
These things will eventually be understood.

If I would just take the time to pray . . .
And listen to what God has to say.
I could avoid so many mistakes,
As prayer prevents them from taking place.

So, my prayer is, Dear Lord . . .
Help me to listen to You and be in one accord.
One with the Holy Spirit knowing Your will, I pray.
Dear Lord, Give me wisdom, so
You can have Your way.

If any of you lack wisdom, let him ask of God, that
giveth to all men liberally, and upbraideth not; and
it shall be given him . . . . James 1:5 KJV

Dear Lord

Dear Lord,
Come what may . . .
When I pray.
Help me to stand fast,
And finish the task.

Help me not to be afraid . . .
Or to go astray.
Give me courage not to run,
But to stand firm till the job is done.

I turn to you for strength . . .
When I feel weak and things seem bleak.
Sometimes I may feel feeble and scared,
But to run I do not dare.

Keep the devil on the run . . .
With perseverance help me to become,
Your servant, with a child like faith,
By living under your grace.

Help me to face my fears . . .
Draw me near,
In silent prayer.
For I know how much you care.

You care for each of us . . .
All you want is our love and trust.
Believe in the only begotten Son.
It is in Him that our victory is won.

Praise the Lord . . .
Please, Dear Heavenly Father tell me more.
How much you love us through Jesus Christ.
The one and only sacrifice.

Please, Dear Lord . . .
Tell me more,
Of the one I adore.
When I come to the Heavenly Shore.

You say, there will be no more pain or suffering . . .
Only the love of Jesus through the blood's covering.
Embraced in His love from the
Heavenly Father above.
What more could I ask for? Dear Lord . . .

God's Truth and Love

Make known God's word . . .
So it may be heard.
That Christ is Alive
In whom we abide.

Cleansed by His blood . . .
By faith through His love.
Rejoicing in God's gift
In Christ, no longer adrift.

Faithful to God's calling . . .
Bring healing to the hurting.
The cure is in His Word
When the gospel is heard.

Speak the truth in love . . .
Spread the word of God abroad.
Make known His love to all
That Jesus may call.

Your Word is a Lamp to my Feet
and a Light to my Path . . .

Your Word is a lamp to my feet,
And a light to my path.
God gives us His light through His Word.
Your Word is like a staff.

Like the sailors lighthouse beams bright.
God's Word will shine the light,
In preparation for our plight.
He guides us through the night.

Your Word is a lamp to my feet,
And a light to my path.
God gives us His peace through our tests.
The Lord will meet our task.

Your Word is a lamp to my feet,
And a light to my path.
God's Word shows us the way to take.
Have faith in God to ask.

Your Word is a lamp to my feet,
And a light to my path.
God will give us the help we need.
Within His peace and rest.

Your Word is a lamp to my feet,
And a light to my path.
Show us Your ways, with each new day,
Through a faith that will last.

Psalm 119:105

Part V

The Simplest Things

There is so, much to be thankful for . . .
The simplest things in life are expressed even more.
Which add up to the big things in life,
We have choices but sometimes with a price.

Some come easily . . .
We either rejoice by singing.
Or be discouraged over each little incident,
That comes down the pike of being discontented.

It's how we look at things with a thought . . .
Before you know it we are caught.
We get caught up in our attitudes,
Which fills our mind with self gratitude.

How did my thoughts come this far? . . .
What was I thinking of?
It gets to be contagious,
What brought on my aggravation?

It just started out as one simple thing . . .
In my mind it grew bigger and bigger from the beginning.
Life sometimes throws us a curve.
And somehow we become unnerved.

The tongue lashes out . . .
In anger no doubt.
Thinking life is unfair,
Nobody really cares.

Then with time . . .
We begin to whine.
We mumble and complain,
It's hard to explain.

When we know farewell . . .
Our tongue begins to tell.
What is in our hearts,
Our thoughts accepted lies even from the very start.

Jesus made it simple . . .
He does not ask for perfection when we are sinful.
Only, that we believe on the Lord, Jesus Christ.
Repent of our thoughts and our ways in this life.

Yes, there are times . . .
That we become carnal and whine.
With self justification,
It is with Christ we have broken relations.

But we as His children can . . .
Praise God with our lips on one hand.
Then complain in the same sentence,
Out of the mouth comes discontentment.

I seem to realize with each given sign . . .
The matter of fact we can all be unkind.
Forgive us Lord for our inconsistencies,
Bring us back to repentance and Your cleansing.

We cannot do it without You . . .
As our guide through God's word in His truth.
Help us to remember the simplest things,
The joy of remembering that it brings.

For the simplest things . . .
Is what makes the world a better place through believing.
"For all things work together for good to them that love God,
That are called according to His purpose"
through Christ Jesus to whom we belong.

"Old things are passed away . . .
All things become new" in each new day.
We receive the mind of Christ,
When we die to self in this life.

We bring glory to His Name . . .
To be like minded one in the same.
Rejoicing in His love,
In His gentle ways, even as the dove.

Rejoice evermore . . .
"Pray without ceasing."
A love that is heaven bound,
Someday to receive a crown.

Keep believing and confessing with your tongue . . .
Christ is Lord and Savior in song.
The joy that it will bring,
In the simplest things.

James 3, Philippians 4:4, I Thessalonians 5:16-18,
Romans 8:28, II Corinthians 5:17, Romans 10:9-10

It's Great To Be Alive

With Jesus as my Guide

Life was a void without my Savior . . .
Wishing only for the week-ends to get
here to give life a little flavor.
So, I could just have my fun.
Only caring for myself and not really for anyone.

Like the man at sail in a ship going to and fro . . .
With no one to direct from the
helm with nowhere to go.
When the storms came,
I was at a loss with my life being the same.

I felt empty and undone . . .
Asking myself where did I come from?
God used the storms of life to draw me near.
My life was turned inside out, with all kinds of fear.

Out of desperation I called out to the Lord . . .
Please, help me I'm lost, my life is in discord.
The waves are over my head,
I might as well be dead.

God was my only hope . . .
I asked Him to help me cope.
Forgive me Lord for what I have done,
This way just isn't anymore fun.

Jesus took the helm of the ship for me . . .
Peace be still, He says, "I died for you on the tree."
I took your place,
Now you can live under God's grace.

Yes, there are more storms to come . . .
With Jesus at the helm I will cecum.
While in the ship of life,
I have learned to love Christ.

Each day holds a new adventure . . .
With Christ at the helm, my life
is no longer pretentious.
Thank you for giving me life,
I now know Heaven will be my plight.

Taste and see that the Lord is good . . .
Call on His Name if only you would.
Through life's storms there is peace,
Through it all your faith will increase.

God has a plan for each new day . . .
Ask Him to show you the way.
Don't hesitate and don't be afraid,
Christ is the only way.

I look at things differently now . . .
I anticipate each new day and
think to myself, Oh! Wow!
It's Great to be Alive,
With Jesus as my Guide.

If we confess our sins He is faithful and just to forgive us
and to cleanse us from all unrighteousness . . . . 1 John 1:9 KJV

Jesus Is Enough

Who can one turn to when life seems unfair?
How do I face each new day without fear?
Is it a sin to worry about our cares?
How can I know or even question
God? I do not dare.

"Seek ye first the kingdom of God" . . .
There are so many avenues to be aware of.
His word is a lamp to our feet
and light unto our path,
God's word can set the captive free
from sin within the flesh.

Jesus takes the captive and sets him free . . .
No longer in the yoke of bondage
but we are able to see.
It is Jesus who keeps us safe through our tomorrows,
Facing each new day through our trials.

When life is unfair, even tough . . .
He's all we need for, Jesus is enough.

But seek ye first the kingdom of God, and His righteousness;
and all these things shall be added unto
you . . . . Matthew 6:33 KJV

Thy word is a lamp unto my feet, and a light
unto my path . . . . Psalm 119:105 KJV

Stand fast therefore in the liberty wherewith
Christ hath made us free,
and be not entangled again with the yoke of
bondage . . . . Galatians 5:1 KJV

Jesus Is My Redeemer

The glory of the Lord,
Shines through His word.
Salvation to proclaim,
Through His Holy Name.

Cleansed by the blood of the Lamb,
Forever to be His child I am.
I will never be the same,
When into my life He came.

Redeemed, Redeemed.
Hallelujah to the King.
Sitting at the right hand of the Father,
No need to look any further.

Jesus the answer to our prayers,
A God of mercy, for He cares.
Thank you, Lord for Your Son,
Who came to earth and who will return.

For His bride,
All dressed in white.
Finishing the work that He has begun,
Through the only begotten Son.

Part VI

Faced with a Challenge

The beginning of a new generation the power of the television is a Click Away.

In the baby boomers generation there was only black and white television and there was always the ordeal of the rolling screen and not to mention the getting up and the changing of the channels. A few channels to be had. NO CLICK!

Then came out the console T.V. set with the colored screen. Just think colored television. There were no ratings at that time because their were programs like Bozo's Circus, Howdy Doody Time, I Love Lucy and many more family shows that they had for entertainment. But of course there was the hassle of needing to get up and change the channel until you found something and there was also the T.V. Guide if you did not want to change all the channels by the turn of a switch. NO CLICK!

As years went by some people even owned two television sets. Unheard of at that time but we seemed to think we were moving up in the world. You had family shows such as Happy Days, The Walton's, Little House on the Prairie, Andy Griffith but somehow movies with violence and sexually oriented movies were geared towards the adults and got even worse. But Still, NO CLICK!

As the years progressed they developed the smaller T. V. console set with the clicker as a tool to switch through the channels without having to get up to change them. What a revelation. Although we still had our T.V. Guides to help us along. Just the beginning of the CLICK!

Movies and television shows are ten times worse with ratings and the advertisements you need to thumb through to get past them. No more time to set at the table to eat with family and friends. How could of all this happened in such a short period of time in our generation. To become complaisant in our lives and just let everything go by without even realizing where we are for today. CLICK! CLICK!

We seemed to have lost ourselves in a world that is as unrealistic as some of the movies we watch. It crept up on us before we even realized what we were doing. It has been so, engraved into us even as a Christian we just want to set back and relax after a hard days work and sit in front of the T.V. CLICK! CLICK! CLICK!

Grant it there are still some good Christian shows and movies that have come out lately where they are sharing the gospel of Christ in a whole new way. This is a new revelation to this generation. To choose is good. There is an answer to the problem. Click off the television set until you know for sure it is within God's perimeters.

Dear Lord, bring us back to the basics in our lives. Family things to do. Eating at the table with family and friends. Getting to know each other but most of all getting to know our Father in Heaven by spending time with Him. NO MORE CLICK!!!

Disconnect

Watching commercials . . .
Inappropriate previews . . .
Disconnect cable . . .

This is a true story. My husband and I would find
a half way descent movie but the commercials
were appalling. So, we disconnected our cable. We
are enjoying not having unwanted advertisements
thrown at us in commercials. Our computers
are working even better than before.

If I Could Go Back In Time

If one could go back in time . . .
Taking a good look at the years behind.
I would reevaluate my life.
I'd think again and maybe even twice.

There would be a few changes
I would have made . . .
Maybe today there would be a lot less pain.
The consequences that we sometimes face,
Are the results of our own mistakes.

I would have listened to my parents,
their endurance . . .
With a listening ear to their wisdom and experience.
When you treat others with respect,
It is then that you have no regrets.

I also think of the times as a family . . .
Times and events that were timely.
Mom cooking in the kitchen.
Dad working long hours for our provision.

Yes, I have regrets . . .
Yet I know I have been blessed.
Though we had our ups and downs,
I realize there isn't a perfect
family anywhere around.

But if it can be filled with love . . .
With a thankful heart that does,
Remember the good times they cherish,
And to learn from the bad times through caring.

If I could go back in time . . .
I'd take a different attitude, one with gratitude.
Growing is a learning process,
God can take a life that is a mess
and show us what is best.

Dear Lord, "Open our eyes that we might see" . . .
Through Your word, that sets us free,
To be grateful for all things in Christ,
Putting off the old man and
putting on the new for life.

In His Likeness

Before Christ there was the law.
In each life there was the fall.
When Christ came, it took Jesus.
The Son of God's love to free us.

We were born into this life.
With a soul who needed Christ.
When we sin, we will repent.
Please, forgive of our sin.

You set the captive free,
Cleanse us with Your blood.
Give Your Holy Spirit
From Heaven above.

Let our lives shine for mankind.
Give us a life, In His likeness.
Through God's glory in Jesus Christ.
Let us stand, In His likeness.

Mistakes We Make In Life Lessons

We have much to learn . . .
In this life we can discern.
As the Holy Spirit leads,
To show us what we need.

It may not be what we want . . .
Jesus knows our hearts and thoughts.
Our flesh rebels,
At what Jesus asks or tells.

Mistakes can be made by not listening . . .
Or out of ignorance in our decisions.
Sometimes we go around the same mountain,
Time and time again.

Until Jesus leads the way out . . .
With the praises of God in our mouth.
God is faithful to turn our mistakes,
Around for our good and for His Names sake.

Let us not confuse mistakes with sin . . .
Sin is rooted in our pride to win.
Satan will lure us into temptation,
Unless we trust Jesus through His Salvation.

Lord forgive us when we sin,
Correct us when we make mistakes out of indecision.
Give us a listening ear to Your call,
Give us the willingness to learn life
lessens by giving You our all.

Part VII

Morning Awaits

The Bridegroom draws near . . .
I can hardly wait to hear.
My Savior calling me,
He is the one I long to see.

Jesus is preparing us . . .
With the cleansing of His blood.
Crucifying our fleshly desires,
Waiting on Jesus for that very hour.

I want to be prepared . . .
To meet Jesus in the air.
When He calls my name,
Never to be the same.

The wedding bells will ring.
Jesus will give a shout to bring
His bride all dressed in white.
Bridle bells will ring to our delight.

An invitation to a wedding . . .
At the banquet tables setting.
The banquet will be like no other,
Seeing our sisters and brothers.

We will be rejoicing with our King . . .
At the head of the table we will see.
Our Lord and Savior,
The One whom we worship and adore.

It will be a reunion with the young and the old alike
From all stages of life.
The Lord's table all lined with heavenly food.
I know the wedding feast is coming soon.

Let the wedding bells ring . . .
Chiming . . .
Ding Dong, Ding Dong.
A joyous sound in heavenly songs.

Dear Lord, we await Your calling . . .
Our wait turns into longing.
To see You at Heavens Gate.
Our "Morning Awaits"

I Thessalonians 2:19-20
I Thessalonians 3:12-13
I Thessalonians 5:22-24
II Thessalonians 2:1-3
Matthew 22:8-9 (A Parable by Jesus) NKJV

Jesus uses the example of a wedding feast
to prepare us for His coming.

On The Day Of Christ's Birth

On the day of Christ's birth,
He was sent here to earth.
Being born in a manger,
He would soon face much danger.

There was no room in the inn,
He was born in a world of sin.
He was holy and pure,
There would be much to endure.

For the new baby who was born,
His clothing that was to be worn.
Was a blanket of swaddling cloth,
Not luxurious or soft.

It had only just begun,
With the birth of a new born Son.
A new beginning and a new hope for all,
A way back to God after the fall.

Through the birth of a baby boy,
For many it would bring much joy.
For those who will call upon Him,
He promised He would deliver from sin.

A chance to be free from their sin,
In Christ it would all begin.
His promise was to us,
To believe on the Lord Jesus Christ and trust.

He was not only King of the Jews
but King of the gentiles too.
He loved us very much and many
lives He would touch,
He came here to earth . . .
And it all began on the day of Christ's birth.

Set Aside My Pride

Please, Dear Lord,
Help Me To Set Aside My Pride.

It's been awhile, Dear Lord . . .
To say the things that need to be said,
I ask for Your forgiveness instead.
As I kneel down before.

It's because of You . . .
That I can say,
I'm sorry for my sins.
I am the one to blame.

Your mercy is complete . . .
With Jesus on the throne.
Sitting on the right hand of God.
He intercedes.

I have allowed the enemy to distract me . . .
But in my confusion.
I humbly bow before You.
Asking for Your mercy to set me free.

Please, Dear Lord, help me to set aside my pride . . .
As the blood of Jesus cleanses me from within.
Make me white as snow, so that I might know.
That I will be ready when the trumpet blows.

Sing Praises to the Lord our Master

Sing praises to the Lord our Master,
For He brings us joy and laughter.
Lift your hands and sing,
Unspeakable joy He brings.

Sing praises to the Lord our Master,
It's a time to rejoice through laughter.
Open your hearts to Jesus,
Lift Him on high, He's the one who frees us.

Holy is the King of kings,
And Lord of lords.
Pressing to the mark of the goal.
Reaching out to lost souls.

Hallelujah, our Lord is coming,
Bringing the bride of Christ home, singing.
The joy of the Lord brings laughter.
Sing praises to the Lord our Master.

Something to Talk About

There is a lot to talk about in this world . . .
Some things that are irrelevant for sure.
But my favorite thing to talk about,
Is Jesus Christ our Lord, without a doubt.

He's good, loving and kind . . .
Jesus is Lord and always by our side,
And He is worth giving Him our time.
How blessed we are to have Jesus Christ.

He listens to our prayers . . .
When life seems unfair.
I laugh with Him,
I tell Jesus of my sins.

Our gift from God is forgiveness through
Jesus, whom You planted . . .
Please, forgive me when I take you for granted.
Your attentive to my every prayer.
How could I be so unkind or unfair.

Thank you, for all that You are in Christ . . .
The Lord and Savior of our life.
Let me start with You in each new day,
And remember to say thank you, when I pray.

We have many things to talk about . . .
But without a doubt.
I find that the best things in life,
Is to share your heart with Christ.

The Family That Prays
Together, Stays Together

When we think of what God wants from us,
We spend time in God's word to learn about Jesus.
How can we get to know Him better you say?
By reading the word of God as we pray.

Give us a heart to know you,
Help us to know what to do.
Let us please you by our faith,
A faith that will bring us someday face to face.

God ordained the family,
He came to set us free.
Life is sometimes a challenge,
Sometimes God allows it for balance.

He wants to strengthen us in our faith,
To bring us to a special place.
A family united under His grace.
For the family that prays together, stays together.

The Fruit of the Spirit

Love only comes from God
Joy in the Lord comes from His Love
Jesus **Peace** gives us rest
The Lord is **Long Suffering** with us.

His **Gentleness** will heal
In God's **Goodness** He reconciles
Faith keeps us from a fall,
In His **Meekness** we are humbled.

God gives us **Temperance**,
To be crucified in the flesh
We must die to our lusts
Let us live and walk in Jesus.

The Fruit of the Spirit
Is all one in the Lord Jesus
God's love is true to you
Worship Him in Spirit and truth.

Galatians 5:22-25

The Hiding Place

There is a place . . .
That I go to for His grace.
I hide myself in Jesus,
The one who frees us.

In my prayer closet . . .
Is when I feel my closest.
I call upon His name.
It was for us He came.

Jesus shares His word with us . . .
As I meditate on Him in trust.
Jesus is faithful to comfort,
I find Jesus to be honest and up front.

He's never condemns . . .
God through Christ is our best friend.
Under His wings I take shelter,
I feel safe in Jesus as my Savior.

Thank you Lord for listening . . .
It's because of You that I can believe again.
No matter what comes along,
I find myself in the hiding place of Your arms.

Part VIII

The Son of Man

To expand is to grow . . .
Life has different ways to show.
How life expands itself and flows,
In this world we know.

Facing each new day . . .
Challenges along the way.
For grace is what we pray.
To help the broken in heart not to stray.

Let us stay fixed on Jesus so, we may shine . . .
So, the Lord may say your mine.
How Jesus, prays for our time,
To spread His love to all mankind.

Meditating on God's word . . .
To become more like Him in this world.
Facing our temptations with His sword.
Putting on the armor of God while we surge.

May our hearts expand . . .
In this thirsty land.
May our hunger to know the Lord stand.
In our time on earth as man.

Without Jesus we would die in our sins . . .
Not being able to face ourselves within.
Life would wither up without our Friend,
Knowingly our life would be grim.

He is the real meaning who puts life together . . .
God gives us a life that will measure.
Lord give us a heart that will grow forever,
In You, with growth there are many treasures.

There is nothing in this world that grows . . .
Without the life of Christ so, one may know.
With His light it comes to show,
Our life is intertwined with lessons that flow.

It helps one's life and heart to expand . . .
Faith in the God who helps us to plan.
Our lives with Him so, we in return can stand.
To know Him as the Son of man.

There Will Always Be Trials

There will always be trials to go through in life
there is only one Teacher to help pass every test
by God's word and Spirit, our Lord Jesus Christ.

A life of comfort God's word never promised
but when humbled in spirit and
pliable through Jesus
things become easier when we know He is with us.

As earth's doors are closed, Heaven's
windows are opened
when we receive God's Word and
our wills have been broken;
As we learn to wait on Him, the
more He will strengthen.

When we are accused falsely, is that something new?
It happened to Joseph, to so
many . . . Lord also to You!
When it happens, Lord help us; show us what to do.

The wounds of a friend are so hard to bear!
Even so, we are Yours Lord, and
are under Your care;
Help us live as You taught us, to leave all in prayer.

But not just for ourselves are we taught to pray
Or just for our loved ones and
Christian friends, each day
God's word teaches us more, if
we let God have His way.

For our enemies that hurt us,
for these we should care
For here in the deep things of God lies our cure.
They are enemies no longer when
we lift them in prayer!

God seals every wound and heals all our sores
When His children release all hatred,
and let His love out pour
Bitter roots wither, prejudice dies,
in God's cleansing power.

There will always be trials to go through in life
there is only one Teacher to help pass every test
by God's word and Spirit, our Lord Jesus Christ.

By: Cinda M Carter & Tom Blakely

Tried And Purified

Jesus was tried in the wilderness . . .
After a forty day fast alone with
God to face the task.
Satan tempted Jesus at His weakest moment,
Jesus was tried and tested by Satan
for us to be an atonement.

Satan used the word of God . . .
And took it out of context, this was his plot.
Jesus had no sin in Him,
But Satan still attempted to mislead
Christ so, he could win.

The enemy used three tactics to draw Jesus in . . .
Satan tempted Jesus with the illusion
of bowing down before him.
Through the flesh, the world and the devil,
By trying to bring Jesus Christ down to his level.

Jesus our Lord used the Word of God . . .
Satan quoted the scriptures to
lure our Lord into His plot.
By using Spiritual Weapons along with God's Word,
He won the victory over the devil by
being faithful to His Father our Lord.

After the testing . . .
God sent angels as messengers.
To minister to Him,
And to give Jesus strength from within.

Then Jesus was ready . . .
With the message of God's forgiveness toward man.
He gives us God's peace through Salvation's plan.
Through His commitment to us
we are able to stand.

We too will be tried and purified . . .
Discerning with God's Word, Satan's lies.
Be not deceived by the devils strategies,
For God is faithful to those with
faith in Jesus to believe.

The plan has been fulfilled . . .
Jesus gave His life for us and loves us still.
Their is no greater love than this that a
man lay down His life for His friends.
Because of Christ we have the forgiveness of sin.

Unmerited Favor

God is love . . .
His whole existence
Is one of Holiness.
His mercy comes from above.

When He created mankind . . .
It was out of a desire,
With love we would acquire,
A love so divine.

We have a free will . . .
To choose whom we will serve,
So, in turn.
God wants us to fill.

Our lives with Him . . .
He chose a human race,
To give us a place.
To be His friends.

We didn't deserve the love of our Creator . . .
But God loved us so, much.
Through His unconditional love for us.
He gave us His, Unmerited Favor.

Part IX

The Second Coming of the Lord

The Signs of the Times and the End of the Age . . . Matthew 24:3-14

Whether there is going to be a rapture before the tribulation, I really do not know. I have prayed and asked the Lord for wisdom on this subject and do not quite understand it all. This one thing I do know is that we are to be ready for His coming.

The disciples asked Jesus, "When shall these things take place?" Matthew 24:3 says, "Now as He sat on the Mount of Olives, the disciples came to Him privately, say, "Tell us when these things shall be? And what will be the sign of Your coming, and the end of the age?" (Rephrased)

Jesus goes on to explain in Matthew 24:4-8 . . . He indicated to not let anyone deceive them. He goes on to say, "Their will be many to come in the name of Christ, and will deceive many. You will hear of wars and rumor of wars and for us not to be troubled because of these things, it must be, but the end will not be yet. Nation will rise against nation and kingdom against kingdom." (The things that we are even seeing as of today in our own generation.) "There will be famines, pestilences, and earthquakes in various places and that these would be only the beginning of sorrows." (Rephrased)

(I realize that it has not taken place in our country as of yet but slowly but surely our freedom is being taken from us as Christians to speak of the gospel of Christ in our government by there being a separation from church and state. I do know that our government was founded upon godly principles and when we prosper we sometimes become greedy and immoral in our ways. So, where does that leave us at? A nation that is immoral and denies God will be a fallen nation.) "My Thoughts"

Matthew 24:9-14 So, Jesus goes on to say, "Then we will be delivered up, in the day of tribulation and they will kill us, and we will be hated by all nations for Christ's Name's sake. Some will be offended and betray one another and will hate each other. Then many false prophets will rise up and deceive many. Lawlessness will abound and the love of many will grow cold. But God helps us to realize that they who endure until the end shall be saved. And this gospel will be preached all over the world as a witness to the nations, and then the end will come." (Rephrased)

The Great Tribulation . . . Matthew 24: 15-27

"Therefore when we see the 'abomination of desolation, spoken of Daniel the prophet, standing in the holy place" (whoever reads, let him understand), then let those who are in Judea flee to the mountains and he who is on the housetop not to take anything from his house, and he who is in the field not to go back for his clothes, but woe to those who are with child in those days and who are nursing babies, pray that your flight may not be in the winter or on the Sabbath! For there shall be great tribulation, never seen since the beginning of the world or until this time, no, nor ever will be. Unless those days were not shortened, no flesh would be saved; but for the elects sake those days will be shortened. Then if any says, to you here is the Christ or there He is, do not believe it. For false Christs and false prophets will rise and show great signs and wonders, to deceive even the very elect. See, I have told you before hand. So, as the lightning comes from the east and flashes to the west so, shall the Son of Man be. (Rephrased)

The Coming of the Son of Man . . . Matthew 24:29-31

"Immediately after the tribulation of those days the sun will be darkened, and the moon will not give it's light; the stars will fall from heaven, the powers of heaven will be shaken. Then the sign of the Son of Man will appear in heaven, then all tribes of the earth will mourn, and they will see the Son of Man coming on the clouds of heaven with power and great glory. And He will send His angels with a great sound of the trumpet, and they will gather together His elect from the four winds, from one end of heaven to the other." (Rephrased)

The Parable of the Fig Tree . . . Matthew 24:32-35

"When the fig tree branch has become tender and put forth it's leaves, you know summer is near. When you see these things happening know that it is even at the door. This generation shall not pass away until all these things takes place. Heaven and earth will pass away, but My words will no means pass away." (Rephrased)

No One Knows the Day or Hour . . . Matthew 24:36-44

Jesus says, "The only one to know the day or hour is His, Father in Heaven." "But it shall be as in the days of Noah so, shall the coming of the Son of Man be. Before the flood they were eating, drinking, marrying and giving in marriage, until the day Noah entered the ark, and they did not know until the flood came and took them all away, so also shall the Son of Man be." It says, one shall be taken and the other left. Watch therefore for you do not know what hour the Son of Man is coming." (Rephrased)

We are to be watchful in prayer as we wait on the Lord. I do not pretend to understand it all but I do know that the Lord wants us to be ready for His coming. In the last verse here, Jesus makes it clear "Therefore you also be ready, for the Son of Man is coming at an hour you do not expect." Matthew 24:44 NIV 'Original Verse'

(Sentences and paragraphs in parenthesis are my thoughts on the subject.) "I rephrased some of the verses from the NIV version to shorten the topic, which are in quotation marks, but gave the original Bible verses for references."

A Nation of Fornication

What standards have we set for ourselves?
A nation that only thinks of one's self.
Our own ambitions,
Our own explanations.

No longer are we called a nation of God.
We have decided that we don't need
Him in this world we trod.
We have taken prayer from our schools.
Young people fight out in a dual.

Killing one another for no reason to explain.
Only heartache for the families
who have lost their way.
No more absolutes,
Only what comes with an attitude.

Dear Heavenly Father,
How much more is there to endure.
We live together before marriage,
Because we are afraid commitment is to daring.

In the 1970's more than 70% of
Americans believed in marriage first.
Planning a family after marriage was
known to be the norm by giving birth.
Now 66% of our younger generation thinks
it's okay to live with one another.
Before you even say "I do" with
an attitude of why bother.

Men marrying men,
Women marrying women.
Pushing on us their immoral rights,
Taking our nations rights to fit their life.

God have mercy on us,
Forgive us for being complacent in our thoughts.
By not teaching our young people
absolutes through God's Word,
For letting the inevitable happen before the surge.

In: A Nation of Fornication

Who Does It Hurt?

(Thoughts To Ponder On)

Have you ever really thought
about how God feels? . . .
We as His creation are made in His image but still.
We still don't always take the time of day,
To worship Jesus in His Spirit and truth in this way.

We have emotions . . .
Still even after the fall in our erosion.
There is a void in the center of man,
The fall was not God's original plan.

To redeem us . . .
He sent Jesus.
God took the pain on the cross for our sin,
The sin of self will, living in the
outer shell from within.

How does Satan attempt to distort things? . . .
Of what value to him does it bring.
Really, he could care less about us,
What is all the fuss?

It's about getting even . . .
Even with the one it hurts the most
while in the garden of Eden.
Satan wanted to get back at God
and thought he could boast,
And thought who does it hurt the most?

Who does it hurt? . . .
God so loves man who inhabits this earth.
Brought down with a curse,
It is God who the enemy hurt.

When I sin

When I sin,
In the way I behaved.
There are temptations.
That take me unaware.

Satan draws me in,
Hoping I will sin.
When we face the truth,
Of how we are uncouth.

If being honest with ourselves,
We realize that we have dealt.
With Satan's deceit and temptation.
Then Jesus convicts the sensitive victim.

I realize what I have done,
I've sinned against Your, Son.
I choose to confess my sin.
I repent, I ask You to forgive me from within.

Cleansed by the blood of the Lamb,
Forever His I am.
It's because Jesus died on Calvary.
To set the captive free.

Patient to forgive . . .
My Savior to believe.
I ask Him to forgive . . .
When I sin.

White as Snow

My sins were as scarlet,
Now there white as snow.
Cleansed by the blood of Jesus,
Now to be made whole.

Jesus shed His blood for us,
Faithful to forgive us.
When we repent of our sins,
Ask Him for forgiveness.

It's a joy when we walk with Jesus,
His aim is to have a relationship.
With the ones He created.
God had so much love to share with us.

He wants to make us as His own,
Teaching us His way.
Seeking His will,
As we kneel to Him and pray.

Forever in His presence,
To sing of His salvation,
Cleansed by the blood of Jesus,
Made in His image.

For the glory of God,
Faithful to His own.
A servant of Jesus,
Accepted into His fold.

Never more to be tossed to and fro,
For Jesus leads us.
We are cleansed by the blood of Jesus,
To make us White as Snow.

Ye Must Be Born Again

How can one be born again?
Must he reenter into his mother's womb?
It is the Spiritual Birth,
When one is delivered from the curse.

One man's sin entered into the world.
A pure sacrifice was to be lifted up for our soul.
God had a second plan,
To redeem the fate of man.

We were doomed to die the second death.
Jesus was are ultimate sacrifice for us.
He had done no wrong, nor had sinned.
Yet, Jesus died on the cross then
was raised to live again.

Today we live under God's grace.
Jesus took for us our place.
With His blood, Jesus gave His life.
So, we would not have to face our plight.

A plight far worse than death.
Where there is no place of rest.
A hell with flames of fire never to be quenched.
Where one goes, when there is no repentance.

We didn't deserve His forgiveness . . . .
Jesus our redeemer was sinless.
And delivered us from our sins . . .
For, Ye must be born again.

Salvation

The ending and a new beginning is coming near . . .
God gives us mercy and His determination.
One need not fear.
He made us in His image in this creation.

God is full of love . . .
He made us perfect and without flaw.
His Holy Spirit leads us and is as gentle as a dove.
God made us a free will to choose before the fall.

God gave us His sovereign grace to decide . . .
Whom we would serve?
Do we choose our own way or simply to abide in the Christ?
Satan, is deceitful with temptations and his lures.

One of Satan's first tricks is to get our undivided attention . . .
Adam and Eve had it all,
Of every tree they were free to eat, Satan
lured them with his deceit.
They made their choice and just as God said there came the fall.

God had a backup plan and sent to us His Son Jesus Christ . . .
To cleanse us from all unrighteousness.
When we choose to come to Him.
Jesus delivers and cleanses us from all our sins.

So, we can all be free and to be at liberty,
By sharing God's salvation through the beloved Christ,
He who was willing to pay the ultimate price,
His life.

Let us choose what is right . . .
And that is to give our lives to Christ.

For God so loved the world and He gave His only
Begotten Son that whosoever believes in Him shall not
parish but have eternal life . . . John 3:16 KJV

Epilogue

"Give me a Song"

Give me a song to hum along.

One that makes you smile while going the extra mile.

It puts a spring in one's step while doing one's best.

It gives laughter, one that brings joy to the Master.

Give me a song to hum along.

With the joy of the Lord in hand with the sword.

In Christ there is a song, let us hum along.

Awaken the day, hum along the way.

With the rising of the sun, let's rejoice everyone.

When we face each new day sing in a special way.

Hum, hum, hum along with a song.

We have a choice to rejoice.

Whether we have a song or just want to hum along.

God is there and helps us to share,

His love through Jesus above.

He brings joy to our hearts in every morning as we start.

Looking to rejoice with gladness to chase away the sadness.

When we draw near to our Lord whom we adore,

Then His love shows through as being true.

A faithful God, on our journey we trod.

Facing our trials for the day in Jesus Christ we pray;

"Give us a song to hum along."